LITTLE EXERCISE BOOKS
Brain games for personal wellbeing

EXERCISES FOR
FINDING HAPPINESS

Anne van Stappen

Illustrations Jean Augagneur

The Five Mile Press

The Five Mile Press Pty Ltd
1 Centre Road, Scoresby
Victoria 3179 Australia
www.fivemile.com.au

Copyright © Éditions Jouvence, 2010
English translation copyright © The Five Mile Press, 2012
This edition published 2012
First published 2010 by
Éditions Jouvence, S.A.
Chemin du Guillon 20
Case 184
CH-1233 Bernex
www.editions-jouvence.com
info@editions-jouvence.com

Cover: Éditions Jouvence
Page layout: atelier weidmann
Cover and internal illustrations: Jean Augagneur
Translated into English by Patsy Abott-Charles
Formatting in English translation: Caz Brown

ISBN: 978 1 74300 263 6

Printed in China

Is it possible to cultivate happiness in a world that's becoming more and more stressful, complex and uncertain? When our dull grey sky is so often weighed down with bad news, can we spread enthusiasm and vibrant dynamism, while at the same time being conscious of the realities that surround us?

Yes, and this book invites you to try it.
Together we are going to examine true joy that endures and doesn't conceal adversities within it (depression, resignation, desolation). This subtle joy springs the ability to spot, enjoy, cultivate and

preserve the beauty of life, in yourself and in the world around you. Its roots are in daring to dream and being completely yourself, it strengthens itself in your presence and, in an instant, blooms with the marvel of giving, loving, receiving and being loved, together with respect for yourself and your personal surroundings.

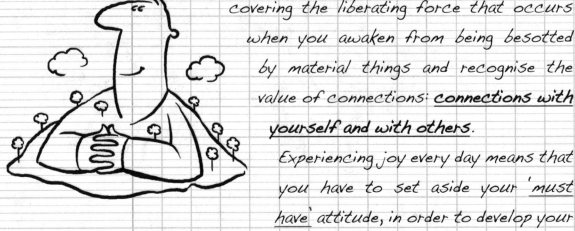

The cultivation of happiness is, above all, understanding that the source of the most stable enthusiasm is found in the living being. It's discovering the liberating force that occurs when you awaken from being besotted by material things and recognise the value of connections: **connections with yourself and with others**.

Experiencing joy every day means that you have to set aside your 'must have' attitude, in order to develop your internal foundations.

4

To do that, let's use the metaphor of cultivating your internal garden! And even though we lead hyperactive lives, let's slow down our rhythm a little, to let us become aware of the living beings that we are and exchange quantity for quality.

In the times in which we live, where excessive material-ism threatens the integrity of our space and has failed in its efforts to give us the prosperity we yearn for, cultivating happiness raises the social stakes. And it's paramount for the self that each one of us is able to cultivate the seeds of our happiness.

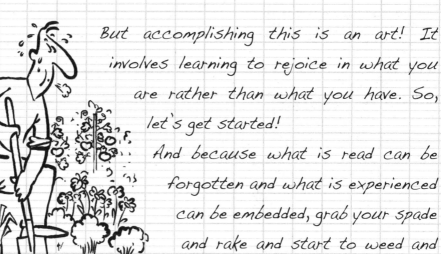

But accomplishing this is an art! It involves learning to rejoice in what you are rather than what you have. So, let's get started!

And because what is read can be forgotten and what is experienced can be embedded, grab your spade and rake and start to weed and dig your plot of land ...   5

First of all, let's define together the various forms that happiness can take:

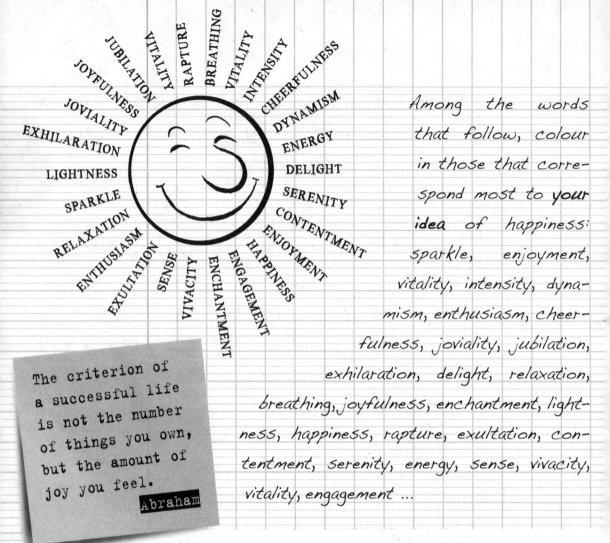

JUBILATION VITALITY RAPTURE BREATHING VITALITY INTENSITY CHEERFULNESS JOYFULNESS DYNAMISM JOVIALITY ENERGY EXHILARATION DELIGHT LIGHTNESS SERENITY SPARKLE CONTENTMENT RELAXATION ENJOYMENT ENTHUSIASM HAPPINESS EXULTATION SENSE VIVACITY ENCHANTMENT ENGAGEMENT

Among the words that follow, colour in those that corre- spond most to **your** **idea** of happiness: sparkle, enjoyment, vitality, intensity, dyna- mism, enthusiasm, cheer- fulness, joviality, jubilation, exhilaration, delight, relaxation, breathing, joyfulness, enchantment, light- ness, happiness, rapture, exultation, con- tentment, serenity, energy, sense, vivacity, vitality, engagement ...

The criterion of a successful life is not the number of things you own, but the amount of joy you feel.
Abraham

Then read aloud the words you have coloured in, at the same time feeling the energy that they contain.

6

The object of the exercise is simple: <u>to be well balanced and strong, it's essential to learn and develop a positive state of mind, and this could be your context for life. There's no need to wait for any particular reasons for that to happen.</u>

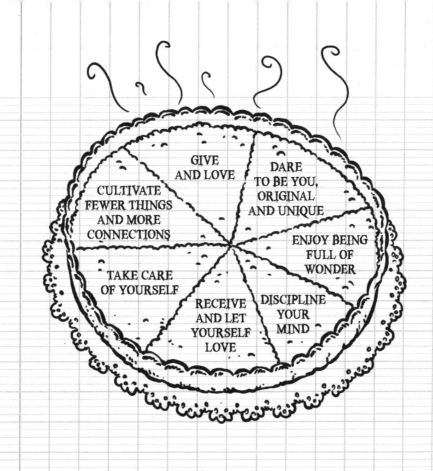

Take care of yourself

Make a list of ten things that stimulate your happiness and ten things that dampen it (situations, thoughts, etc.).

Start by delighting in all those things that stimulate your happiness.

7

Savour them slowly, one by one!

What comes from me

What stimulates my happiness

What comes from the outside

What crushes it

What is a mixture of both

8

Then, taking a look at what dampens your happiness, sincerely ask yourself the following questions:

Is it possible for me to take action over the external things that crush my happiness?

> ☛ For example: I'm not strong enough to be a truck driver!
>
> ▶ But what if I think of doing some body-building sessions?
>
> ☛ For example: My boss complains about me but never gives any concrete reasons for it.
>
> ▶ But what if I ask him to give me three elements that he would like to see changed in my attitude?

Is it possible for me to take action over things that ruin my happiness?

> ☛ I get hypersensitive over nothing.
>
> ▶ And if I find out about how to overcome these states of mind?

Make a note of the possible action you could take for each matter (situation, event, thought ... that can crush your happiness.

And to stimulate your spirit of adventure, let Marc-Aurèle inspire you ...

Now, outline your **ideal day**, the sort of day that brings you joy: use of time, creativity, actions, relationships, recreation, etc. See if this joy depends primarily on what you **are**, **do** and/or **feel**, or on what you **consume** or **possess**.

Ask yourself if, from today, it is possible there is an attitude you could adopt that would make this day correspond to **one** of the aspects of your ideal day. For example, if in your ideal day you like to mix with friendly people, you could decide to go to a public place and smile at a few people whom you don't know. There's a possibility that one of them might return your smile.

Attention! It's never easy to change your habits, but it will be worth it for your life. It's time to develop the art of the good life. **It can be learned, you just need to decide to learn it.** Once you've decided to transform your life, it will be easy to learn how to do it.

10

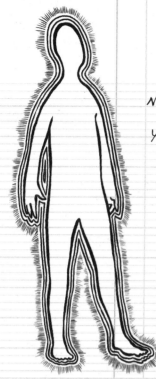

Now, let's look at what is meant by taking care of yourself. But, basically, what is this SELF?

Many traditions think that a human being is composed of four bodies: the physical body, mental body, emotional body and spiritual body. (Some think that there are seven bodies, but that's not the subject of our discussion.)

To be on form, our physical body has to have rest, care and joy.

Do you take the time to:

THE PHYSICAL BODY

PROTECT IT?

EXERCISE IT?

LISTEN TO IT?

RELAX IT?

CARE FOR IT?

GIVE IT HEALTHY FOOD?

LET IT HAVE QUALITY SLEEP?

GIVE IT PLEASURE?

11

MAKE IT WORK?

Or do you think that your body <u>has</u> to work and that you'll do that later?

As your day unfolds, do you ever 'pause', to reflect? To stop reflecting? To regenerate yourself when your energy is low? Or do you stop only when you really can't do any more? Or only when the day is finished?

If your performance slows down, is it your habit to have a coffee or a stimulant to boost you? Do you drink alcohol or take tranquillisers in the evening to relax?

Do you think that you give yourself enough time for relaxation each day?

Do you spend most of your day feeling tense about something you want to achieve?

Do you treat yourself as we treat our land, by exhausting it from intensive farming, poisoning it with fertiliser and weed killers?

Of the 1440 minutes in a day, how many do you spend being attentive to yourself?

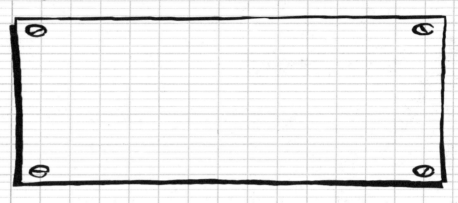

Consider these questions. What do you think of your answers? Are they satisfactory or worrying?

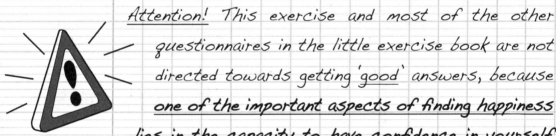

Attention! This exercise and most of the other questionnaires in the little exercise book are not directed towards getting 'good' answers, because **one of the important aspects of finding happiness lies in the capacity to have confidence in yourself** and develop your own internal radar.

So, while the answers to your questions give you temporary peace, learning to live with the questions to discover your own resonance will give you a 13 calmness and long-lasting stability ...

Observe how you feel about having your own answers to these questions as your only reference.

Here are several sentences to contemplate and colour in:

Your cells know, do you take time to listen to them and follow what they say to you?
Marie Pier Charron

To live joyfully, you must overcome the tension of watchfulness.

Everything in life is fluid.
Movement allows energy to circulate.
When energy is blocked, illness occurs.

You dig your grave with your knife and your fork.
Gurumayi Chidvilasananda

Sometimes it's when I stop that I progress most.

Speed affects our psyche and makes us ill ...
Living more slowly allows the renewal of more intense connections, including connections with the slowest of us and the oldest of us in life.
Pascale d'Erm

14

The mental body is constituted by our thoughts. The mind is made to think. That's not a problem in itself. The problems arise, or don't, according to the way we process our thoughts to represent reality or not, and to which we attach ourselves or not.

Therefore, our life results from the way we direct our thoughts and our beliefs (a belief is a thought that one is very attached to over a long period of time).

For example, if you think, 'I'm nothing and I will never get the job I dream of!', you show your-self as unstable and lacking in self-assurance. Having this belief will lower your chances of being given the job. If you're not chosen for the job, the belief will comfort you with the idea that, 'I know I'm nothing', and so a vicious circle begins ...

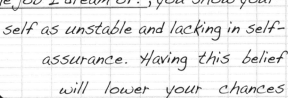
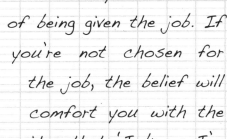

15

Exercise

Flush out <u>one</u> of your negative beliefs concerning yourself or life and look for what you do to show that it's true. This exercise is complex and could take some time because our beliefs don't like to be unmasked.

For example: <u>I'm shy and I don't know how to express myself</u>. Because you believe that, it makes you afraid, you avoid speaking, you judge yourself and that makes you very reserved; your paralysis reinforces your shyness and your awkwardness, and consequently proves the validity of your belief.

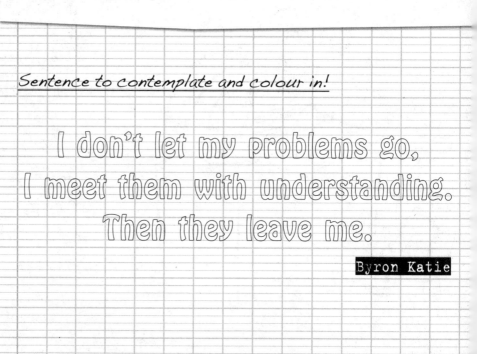

Sentence to contemplate and colour in!

I don't let my problems go,
I meet them with understanding.
Then they leave me.

Byron Katie

16

The emotional body: our emotions reflect the colour that represents life within us from moment to moment. Whether they are pleasant or unpleasant depends on whether we are conscious of them and accept them, because:

☞ If an emotion is pleasant, and you allow yourself to feel it to the full, your vital energy and happiness will grow.

☞ If an emotion is unpleasant, accepting what it feels like without identifying it enables you to hit the bottom. From there you will find the necessary impulse to come up again.

☞ If you refuse to feel what is stirring inside you, you refuse to let life move around you.

☞ If you accept what you are feeling, life will move around you and that will strengthen your ability to experience and to be alive.

Our emotions are neither good nor bad. Our difficulties don't come from our emotions, but from the thoughts that we associate with our experience of life. For example: I'll be worried if I don't get the job that's vital for me. But the problem arises when you say: 'I'll never get anywhere; I'm a good for

17

nothing.' These thoughts engender other disagreeable emotions in you that diminish your energy and happiness. That will stop you from bouncing back and overcoming the difficulty.

Difficult exercise ...

... and so it's optional! Read and listen to your internal radar to see if it's right for you to do it.

The next time that you come up against a difficulty and you feel an emotion and/or a feeling that's unpleasant, don't struggle against it. Feel what you are experiencing in your heart and body, without thinking what it might be! Just simply accept the emotions/feelings for what they are: life moving around in you.

For example, if you're angry, feel the anger; perhaps you feel your jaw tighten, your breathing becomes uneven, your heartbeat quickens? Accept it for what it is.

Then, try to identify the thoughts that come to you, according to their context.

If you become conscious of your thoughts, you will have taken a big step, because you can decide to distance yourself from your anger.

I'M ANGRY

THERE'S ANGER IN ME

In this exercise, frequent repetition of which will bring great rewards, it is essential to distance yourself from the negative emotion. To do that, instead of thinking, 'I'm angry, I'm violent', it would be better to substitute with 'I'm holding a lot of anger inside me' and see the anger as being a thing in you, but not **essentially** you. This will allow you to hold a position as an observer of your life.

19

THE SPIRITUAL BODY

The spiritual body is a presence that exists behind our emotions and our thoughts. It can really shine when our minds are calm and our emotions have been accepted and transformed.

There is a silent observer in each of us that functions as a witness to how we conduct our lives. From this we can recognise our emotions and manage them, and we can turn on the light to see the unconscious beliefs that govern us. When you move from an attitude of doing to one of being, and take a moment for yourself, that will open the space your spiritual body needs to extend itself.

> What makes us rejoice, awakens us to our true nature.
>
> Eckhart Tolle

The seeds of our happiness come from our ability to be present in ourselves (to be able to observe ourselves). This presence makes us conscious and our joy depends on our level of consciousness.

20

The presence in oneself, or full consciousness, is the ability to turn one's attention to the internal self at any time, with curiosity, kindness and without judgement or expectation of anything. To do this, it is sufficient to observe the conduct of one's life in any moment.

Christophe André

Breathing is a bridge between body and soul.
Gurumayi Chidvilasananda

In the course of a day, do you have any idea of the number of moments when you live automatically, without being really conscious?

21

Now, make sure you're sitting comfortably with your back straight but flexible and your feet flat on the floor. Notice your breathing. Let it function naturally. Feel the air that enters and leaves your lungs. Open yourself to what happens within you: wellbeing, agitation, impatience, sleepiness etc. Simply accept what's there. With each breath, become aware of your inhalation and exhalation. Little by little allow a tiny instant to develop between one cycle of inhaling and exhaling and the next.

If you can, empty your mind of all thought and indeed all attendant emotion ...

It's essential to do this daily; at the beginning it will be only be for about five minutes, but after a few weeks' practice your daily encounter with yourself will be about twenty minutes. If you find you experience stress, mental agitation or weariness from this practice, this is completely normal: going into yourself is unsettling because you don't know what you're going to find there, because you're frightened that there's nothing there, because your ego loses its control little by little and suggests that you're doing all this for nothing ...

Persevere, because it's necessary to reduce this stubbornness in you in order to accept yourself.

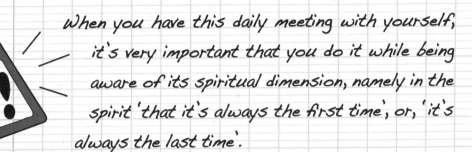

When you have this daily meeting with yourself, it's very important that you do it while being aware of its spiritual dimension, namely in the spirit 'that it's always the first time', or, 'it's always the last time'.

To profit from the practice of full consciousness, you must do it consistently and with effort. After several weeks you will feel better, physically and emotionally; notably your good humour, calmness and creativity will be stimulated and your general body health will be boosted.

23

Above all, don't say, '_I'm going to try it_'; do it!

Here's a little anecdote to encourage you: imagine you're in a plane that is about to land in Melbourne, and you hear the flight attendant make the following announcement: 'Ladies and gentlemen, fasten your seatbelts, we're going to **try** to land'.

What would you feel? Doubtful about the success of the landing, or not?

Well, don't try, do it!

ladies and gentlemen,
fasten your seatbelts,
we're going to
try to land!

Dare to be original and fully yourself, dare to have dreams

Live according to your personal and unique plan. Gather your courage and confidence, to accomplish without detours that to which you aspire. The world needs your joy and you will only find this in the realisation that you are truly you.

Posez-vous ces questions :

MY DARING

	A LITTLE	OFTEN	ALWAYS	NEVER
Am I faithful to myself?	☐	☐	☐	☐
To my values?	☐	☐	☐	☐
To my likes?	☐	☐	☐	☐
Do my actions lead me to what I deeply desire?	☐	☐	☐	☐
Do I dare to be different from what people expect of me?	☐	☐	☐	☐
Have I made room for originality in my life?	☐	☐	☐	☐

DARE TO BE ORIGINAL AND FULLY YOURSELF

25

☞ If your answers are placed
between never and a little,
describe in writing a con-
versation or a moment, step by step as it unfolds, when
you were not being in yourself, and do the same for an
occasion when you were fully in yourself.

☞ How did that happen?

☞ Then play the two scenarios in front of a mirror,
watching your state of mind in each version and ... enjoy
yourself! After all, it's only a mirror — for the moment!

☞ If there's a lot of difference between your two descrip-
tions, take a moment to reflect on the reasons for them
that strike you at this point of knowing yourself.
Perhaps you might decide to change certain aspects of
your current life a little, to have the courage to speak
of this first with those who are close to you. Make
sure these changes equally affect yourself and your
relationships with others.

☞ Note here your observations, from your first tiny step.

DARE TO HAVE DREAMS

If you dream about something, you light a fire within yourself and make a connection with the energy of life; that will make you very attractive!

As soon as possible, go outside with your exercise book. Go to a park, a forest, the country ... Walk slowly **27** and breathe deeply. Open your eyes and look around you, listen to the sounds, smell the scents, touch or stroke anything that takes your liking and benefit from the moment. Contemplate at what point does nature completely fulfil itself. Then, sit down to listen to your inner life.

Ask yourself:

What calls to me in my life?

What do I truly want?

Will I let myself attain that, one day?

List a few real actions to do in order to attain what you want. Even if the list doesn't seem realistic to you, give yourself time to write it.

Commit yourself to doing at least one action listed during the next week.

Describe this action here. Also note the date you will do it and how you're going to do it.

It's better to have big dreams that aren't attained than to have small ambitions achieved without flair.

Enjoy, experience gratitude, be filled with wonder

ENJOY
BE FULL OF WONDER
BE THANKFUL

Colour in the text below and
fill it with your energy.

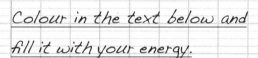

From small pleasures to great aspirations, the thing that makes me deeply joyful is the knowledge of enjoying, cherishing and recollecting that the beautiful and the good exist in my life.

SAVOUR

Let's take a fruit that you like to eat.

We're going to choose an apple.

1. Inhale then exhale deeply several times.

2. Take the apple and wash it in a thin stream of water. Listen to the noise of the water. Watch it slide down the fruit, smell its freshness on your hand and its sweetness ... It is precious! Then, sit down, put the apple on a plate and look at it closely: what colour is it? What's its shape?

3. Then take it in your hands. Is it soft, rough, heavy, light? Take time to be completely aware of what you are doing.

4. Inhale its scent. Stay very much in the present; don't make comparisons with other moments, even if past memories invade you.

5. Cut the apple in quarters and peel it if you wish. Pay attention to the knife you use to cut and peel the fruit, listen to the sound of each slice of the apple. Feel the damp flesh on your fingers. Look at its colour.

6. Slowly bite the first mouthful. Feel the taste and the texture of the flesh, enjoy the juice that fills your mouth and mix it with your saliva.

7. The apple breaks up in your mouth; gently swallow this first piece.

Now look at each apple quarter with the eyes of your heart. Think of everything that has happened to bring this fruit to your house so that you could eat it. The tree on which it grew, the soil in which the apple tree grew, the people who harvested it, the country where this happened. Imagine the whole chain that has been orchestrated to bring the apple to you, to nourish you. Think of where you bought it. Similarly, think of your plate, your cutlery, your chair ... and then feel your gratitude for the abundance of life that, here, has brought you a simple apple. For that, accept and experience each one of the many facets of your sensations and feelings.

If your thoughts take you away from your gratitude, return to listening to your five senses.

Value the time it takes you to do this exercise completely. Do you think it has been a waste of time? Or have you enjoyed this slow sampling?

What have you learned?

If, in any situation, you wanted to strengthen your gratitude for something life has offered you and/or if you want to express this to somebody, it is very powerful, as much for you as for the person you are speaking to, to go over the three stages of Non-Violent Communication, as follows:

1. Note or name an action or gesture that makes you feel good.
2. Identify and name the need that was met following the action in question.
3. Feel and speak your feelings, while replaying them.

Example: When you listened to me about my sadness due to my separation, that satisfied my need to be understood and recognised. And when I think of that, I am moved and full of gratitude for your friendship.

HAVE A SENSE OF WONDER

Think of three brief moments you experienced today and seek their beauty.

For example: the welcoming look from a shopkeeper, a glimpse of blue sky, a new positiveness, the song of a bird, and nothing's too small ...

The aim is to be filled with wonder, not to bemoan.

Joy is everything. To know it is to have it.

Confucius

Our joy depends on our ability to live joyful moments in ourselves. *+ to be MFy about it* More, we experience these moments deeply and our brain becomes used to recognising and handling them. Our wellbeing increases with recognition and managing these positive states of mind. Joy is the sum of our wellbeing and the consciousness of wellbeing.

Christophe André

Cultivate a positive state of mind → BE grateful — KEY

Everything to which I pay attention grows.

For two minutes, submerge yourself in a recent, happy memory. Feel what you experienced, relive your sensations and sample them, and do the same for your feelings. Use your five senses to expand this moment to its fullest. What has this exercise given to you?

And if you started a good news diary, how would you describe this moment?

MY GOOD NEWS DIARY

33

Discipline your mind

But how do you do it on days when everything is fraught, and/or you haven't any energy to accomplish these changes? Well yes, if everything is fraught or painful, it will be much more difficult to change your habits. If you're experiencing some distress, read the following five sentences before addressing aspects of personal discipline. <u>Colour in the sentence(s) of your choice</u> and promise yourself to do some reading about it/them as soon as you have the momentum and strength to work with <u>perseverance in</u> your internal world.

Five sentences for days of distress
(extracts from Don't Walk if You Can Dance)

The night is always darkest
before the dawn.

Strawberries that have been exposed to the greatest cold have more flavour than the others.

When pain is completely accepted, it is transformed.

The most important thing is your attitude. Changing that costs nothing. When you change your attitude, the situation changes.

Try to do what you like doing if you can, and enjoy it. Sometimes, that consists of breathing and feeling the air pass through your lungs ...

35

Now, compose a sentence or think of a belief that could come to fruition and that would help you to be joyful. Then read it every day with courage and openness until you begin to believe that it will eventually happen.

For example: **I know I'm difficult to love!**

When your life is easy and pleasant, it's important to develop your ability to discipline your mind, so that it becomes a habit that will support you in challenging moments.

Here are some exercises to help you to be positive, firm, and even joyful when you encounter difficult times.

P. F. J

BECOME CONSCIOUS OF YOUR THOUGHTS

Becoming the observer of your thoughts helps you to take a step back when faced with the difficulties of daily life. It's essential not to let yourself be radio-controlled by your thoughts! We create our own hell or paradise according to how we manage our minds. Most of the time, when a thought occurs, we surf over it without taking notice, and we find ourselves carried away by a current of ideas that are often negative

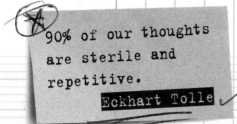

90% of our thoughts are sterile and repetitive.
Eckhart Tolle

and unproductive. It's an enormous advance to achieve and become aware of our automatic mind.

BEEP
BEEP
BEEP

ALARM 5 MIN

Exercise

Set an alarm to go off in five minutes.

Settle yourself comfortably and close your eyes. Take two or three deep breaths and note your thoughts, without judging or analysing or following them. Look at them and let them simply be there. Consider them like clouds that are passing across the sky. Don't try to get on them!

If you find a state of peace inside you, enjoy it. If your mind is agitated, accept it with kindness.

C . G . T.

That said, it's possible that due to this exercise you have become aware of the black thoughts that **37** contaminate your spirit ... Then you will perhaps desire to change them.

This leads us to:

Our minds adore judging, analysing, diagnosing, comparing, evaluating, criticising, pondering, fulminating, complaining, etc. If you become aware of the cost of carrying on like this, you'll really want to let go of them.

Non-violent communication is a method of communicating that enables us to tackle our relationships while remaining close to ourselves and in accordance with our humanity. It excels in helping us to change our black ideas, together with their associated negative mental states, and we can try to discover the dream that they so badly misrepresented.

Thus, <u>what I judged myself to be becomes what I aspire to, and what I wanted from you becomes what I want</u>.

38

For example:

☞ Black idea: <u>in spite of my diet, I splurged this week and put on a kilo. I couldn't help myself!</u>

This type of thought bulldozes our energy and makes us want to compensate for our self-deceit with all the sugary things in the fridge that we can get our hands on!

☞ *What I aspire to: I would like to feel confident that my willpower will keep me focused on my objective.*

This thought connects us to something living. In this case, to have confidence that our willpower will stay the course. And if you focus your attention on what you want, your energy will revive and it will be much easier to find the courage to keep hold of and look for a solid way to achieve the objective.

CHANGING FROM 'I MUST' TO 'I CHOOSE'

Happiness and joy come from an attitude in which you try to link yourself to underlying reasons for which you accomplish things. So, our liking for doing these things grows.

Once you've become aware of your thoughts, **you have the choice to decide how and what to think**. And this is fundamental because our thoughts engender our state of mind.

N.B. - X

39

As it's much nicer to do things with fervour than because you have to, your energy will be lighter if, instead of forcing yourself to do _what you 'should' do_, _you connect to what you choose to do because you_ _'want' to do it_ ... This is a sort of discovery, that 'I choose' is hidden behind the '_I must_'.

Exercise

Note here an activity that you feel you have to do. Then write the met needs and the unmet needs for this.

Met needs	Unmet needs

Before doing anything, try to connect yourself to the met needs through the means of accomplishing them. You will be more positive and lighter in carrying out your business.

For example: <u>I **have** to cook for my family.</u>
Here, you can imagine that the met needs are those of sustenance, taking care of your family and giving them pleasure ... and that the unmet needs are those of resting, relaxing, lightness, and being pampered yourself ...
You may think that because you don't get to relax, that makes the task much worse, or, you can equally decide to give yourself a more pleasant life by connecting to the pleasure of giving and taking care of your family.

▸ <u>I **choose** to take care of my family and look after their sustenance.</u>
AND I ALSO COMMIT MYSELF to giving time to my needs of relaxation at another time!!!

<u>41</u>

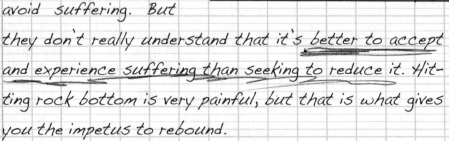

Human beings long for joy and peace of mind. Everyone wants to avoid suffering. But they don't really understand that it's better to accept and experience suffering than seeking to reduce it. Hitting rock bottom is very painful, but that is what gives you the impetus to rebound.

Look back at the optional exercise on page 18. Is now a good moment for you to do it? If your internal radar says yes, the next time a painful emotion strikes you, accept it. Then focus your attention on the part of your body where the pain is. Even if a pain is emotional,

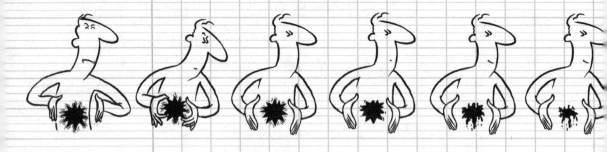

it shows itself physically. Does it have a shape, a colour, a texture, a weight? Accept it without fighting it. Concentrate and breathe calmly in the area of your pain. Let go and let the pain dissolve. Don't do anything to restrict its dissolving! Don't try to make whatever it is right. It is a process that improves little by little, sometimes even without you knowing it.

When you plant a seed of bamboo in the soil, you see nothing for some time. And then suddenly, in an instant, the bamboo shoots up and rises several metres high. For us, perseverance achieves the same miracles that the sun and the rain do in nature.

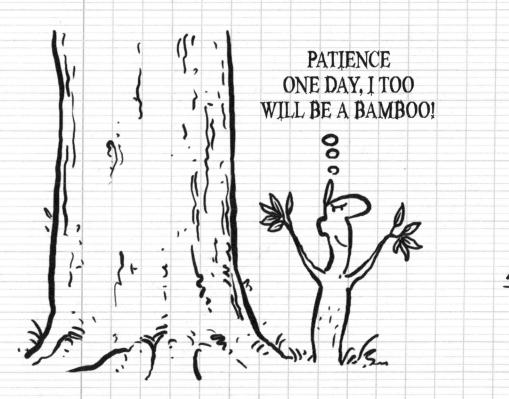

PATIENCE
ONE DAY, I TOO
WILL BE A BAMBOO!

DEVELOP THE SKILL OF 'COMPARTMENTALISING'

Learning to live one thing at a time, confident that what you've put on hold won't suffer much, needs specific training.

When I walk, I walk, when I eat, I eat, when I work, I work, and when I'm with my family, I'm completely there!

Now, answer the following questions:

☞ Do I manage to free myself from professional worries when I'm with my close family?

☞ Can I concentrate on my work when I have other worries?

☞ Which parts of my life do I succeed in compartmentalising?

☞ Which parts is it most important to manage?

44

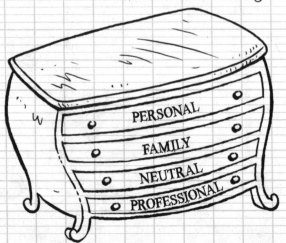

PERSONAL

FAMILY

NEUTRAL

PROFESSIONAL

To develop the skill of separating different parts of your life, it's a good idea to give yourself a neutral space between two different activities. For example, you could decide to stop for a while, a moment of pause, even if it's very brief, instead of rushing headlong into the next activity. If you are on a journey between two places, it can help you to have closure with the former in order to concentrate totally on the new.

Put another way, when you arrive home you could think of saying to your partner that you need a moment of solitude, before participating fully with him/her.

Describe here the neutral space that you are going to put, if necessary, between two parts of your life. And tell people of your intention.

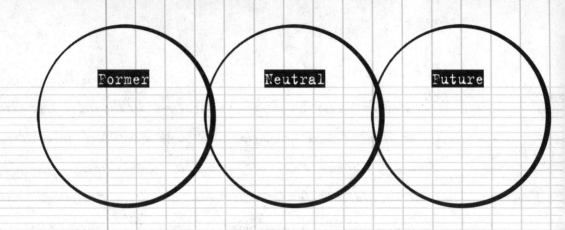

Former   Neutral   Future

Draw or describe in each of the three circles two activities that you have trouble controlling, because of
worries, problems, stress ... and which tend to recur in
your world. Put in the middle circle a symbol of what
you're going to develop to make a transitional space
that will allow you to 'clock off' while remaining fully
aware of what's happening around you.

For example: You are a personal assistant and as the
day goes on so the pace of your work increases. You
leave work strained, stressed, exhausted. Your next
activity often consists of collecting your children
from after-school care as quickly as possible ... What
can you do to be able to welcome them in the least
stressed and most relaxed way possible? Could you
take two minutes alone in your car, just to breathe and
'pause'? Or, could you wait for a moment to rediscover
your internal peace of mind, your own rhythm, for

example, watching the clouds pass overhead? Don't try to find something complicated to do, just try to restore a calmness in yourself, to unlock yourself from your cares.

Find **your** own method, and then try it out to see if it works for you.

The strongest gift in experiencing the joy of life is learning to feel good even when everything around you is going badly. Feeling bad cuts you off from your potential action, except if you search out the unmet needs that give rise to unhappy feelings, you can then examine what action can be undertaken to satisfy them.

Whilst an uncomfortable state of mind is borne passively, nothing will help change the bad situation.

If you want to change your life according to your desires, you have to develop the ability to feel now as if you were already in the life you dream about for tomorrow. Because what you will be tomorrow depends on what you feel today.

David Komsi

47

Difficult exercise ...

... to be repeated very often:

Think of an aspect of your life (not too complex) that preoccupies you. Identify your uncomfortable feelings regarding this aspect.

Ask yourself how you would feel if the problem were resolved.

Make yourself feel this in anticipation. Immerse yourself fully in it!

For example: you've lost your spectacles. You are anxious and/or furious. If you find them, you'll be calm, won't you? Well then, decide to be calm right now, even when you are searching everywhere for the specs!

Having the ability to choose your state of mind enables you to be independent of both good and bad things.

If your happiness is independent of good things, their absence won't make you unhappy.
David Komsi

By way of relaxation, answer the following questions
as ture (T) or false (F):

1. Experiencing joy stimulates the immune
    system. ⬛T ⬛F

2. Negative and positive emotions are
    contagious. ⬛T ⬛F

3. Too much pain, like too much joy, in a
    single stroke stresses the body. ⬛T ⬛F

4. Happiness isn't acquired once and for all;
    it's a discipline of life to be cultivated. ⬛T ⬛F

5. One is joyful or gloomy; that's the way
    it is, it's a question of temperament and
    it can't be changed. ⬛T ⬛F

6. A moderate positive state of mind is
    beneficial for physical and emotional health. ⬛T ⬛F

7. Alcohol makes you happy. ⬛T ⬛F

8. Alcohol makes you depressed. ⬛T ⬛F

9. Happiness depends more on what you have
    than what you are. ⬛T ⬛F

10. Sports activities have an antidepressant effect
    because they stimulate the endorphins. ⬛T ⬛F

11. Managing your emotions will give more
    happiness than possessions and self-pleasure. ⬛T ⬛F

Receive and give love

RECEIVE

It's often more difficult to receive than to give.

You need to remove the cap on the petrol tank, in order to fill up the tank.

Have you removed your cap so the tank can be filled with what has been given to you? Or are you afraid that you will have to reciprocate, or that you don't deserve it, or that it will be improper if you are truly happy, or of being manipulated, bought off, etc.

Do you allow yourself to enjoy the gifts of life or are you reserved about taking daily pleasures?

Be on the lookout, because the present is now!

Very soon, you will no longer be able to savour the same joy that you can savour now!

Here is an essential exercise, which should be practised without restraint, many times each day! The next time someone does something for you (for example, lets your car go first; yes, it can happen!), take a moment to breathe, slow down (not so much your car as your internal rhythm!) and cherish what was given to you. See whether or not it's habitual or easy for you to receive.

Note here things that you have become aware of.

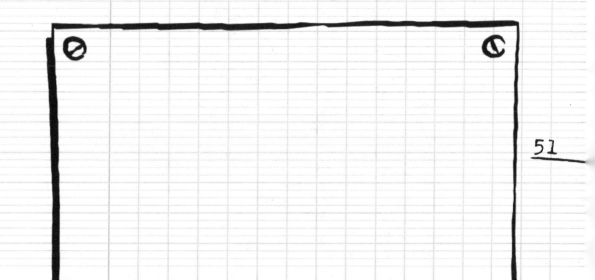

Love opens us and, very often, we long for it, but if it comes knocking we don't reach out and welcome it. Especially if we have been wounded and have become distrustful, cautious, closed ...

Also, love makes us joyful and enthusiastic!

Which is it for you?

Do you accept love freely when it's there?

To choose love is to choose joy.
Marie Pier Charron

52

Loving and giving

LOVE Love is an internal state that depends more on who it comes from than its object. When this love is firmly established in us, it shows itself obviously and very spontaneously in many ways. To cite a few: the free gift without expectation of return (of oneself, one's time, possessions ...), preservation of life, desire to praise the beauty of life, working to develop conscience.

The important thing is to love loving. Not to love because ... The love which we need is that which exists already within us and which seeks to express itself. One chooses love by opening oneself to the part of us where it already lives. From this space real beauty and pure joy emanate.

Marie Pier Charron

A universal law first above all others: the law of fellowship, of love. For the Greeks, fellowship is positivism, love of life, kindness.

53

One can therefore be in love ... even without having lovers!

Exercise: Recall an instance of love and then silently send it out to people around you, even if you don't know them.

Practise this exercise regularly. It will increase tenfold your ability to love.

Finally, it's obvious that love is good to have ... but it is less known that it also improves your health.

54

<u>Here's an illustration</u>: a study was done on babies born to women in prison. In the study some infants had been left in prison with their mother, without having any care or hygiene. Other babies had been taken from their mothers, but had benefitted from care and hygiene. The health balance of these infants showed that those in the first group (left in prison with the mothers but without care) were in better health and had a higher immunity than those in the second group. From this one can deduce that love is a favourable factor in health.

GIVE

<u>Sentences to colour in</u>

What does it matter that I exist
if I don't contribute to making
a better world?

55

Each time I give,
I make a space to receive.

A blind man was trying to get on a train. He struggled on arriving at the platform. A worker noticed him and put down his tools to go and help him. A third person watching this was moved and touched to see such joy on the face of the blind man as well as on that of the worker!

The kindness of the worker increased the wellbeing of everybody, including the observer.

Do you remember the last time when you offered something to someone (it could be your time, an action, a present, a meal, a smile ...). Describe here what you did, your feelings at the time of doing it, the needs that were satisfied for you and for the person whom you helped.

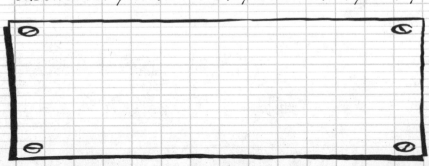

Then observe what you feel
now in recalling the incident.
Did it brighten up your life?
If yes, then here's another
exercise to examine:
Imagine a surprise that you could give someone this
week, whether you know the person or not. If that
intimidates you or makes you afraid, encourage yourself
by remembering that he who doesn't overcome one fear
per day doesn't learn the lesson of life ...

For example, you could buy a flower and put it in front
of the entrance to a flat in your building. Or you could
offer a neighbour a bowl of delicious soup that you've
just made. Or you could compliment the salesperson
who has just served you in a shop ...

Having done this harmless little exercise, you could
make it a daily practice. Also explore the thing you like
doing best: giving surprises to someone you don't 57
know, or giving unexpected attention to those close
to you.

If you act on impulse, it's feasible that the happiness of giving a surprise or of pleasing someone will delight you much more than the person to whom you give it. If this isn't the case, then take care of yourself: prepare yourself for attention and surprises, pamper yourself, until the spirit of doing it for others rises in you.

Sentences to colour in

With all gifts it's essential to give and to immediately forget that one has given. One will be much happier if nothing is expected in return and nothing is talked about later.

Among the behaviours on the next page, colour in those that you've developed in the course of this reading this book, or before. Then, choose one of them to which you will pay special attention in the course of the next few days:

action

mental discipline

sense of now

audacity

listening to yourself

listening to your rhythm

receptivity   gift

changing black ideas

care for your life

changing from 'I must' to 'I choose'

love   relaxation

choice of state of mind

originality

skill of compartmentalising

care for your body

59

Move from the cult of material possessions to that of connections

> If you put end to end the amount of tragedy that televised news thrusts upon us in a month, we would see that they all come from a triple fault line: the rupture of man from himself, from others and from the planet.
>
> Patrick Viveret

This exercise book started by exploring the importance of connecting one to one. It finishes by noting the intensity that a link to another person creates in our lives.

If you still need to be convinced, go to a train station platform and scrutinise the faces of people who are saying goodbye and those who are meeting again. Even the most discreet among them are inhabiting life. Intense emotions

take possession of us when our connections have been interrupted or recreated.

If you were to present yourself in a singular and unique way (as if it was the first or last time) to your nearest and dearest, how would you experience your connection with them?

It's now time for us to part ... I hope you have learned that developing your happiness allows you to be calm without tranquillisers, satisfied without possessions, radiant without drugs and drunk without drinking from any other source than yourself.

And to leave us in simple happiness, here's a last story to think about!

One day at dawn in the high mountains, a walker met a shepherd. He asked him:
'What's the weather going to be like today?'
The shepherd calmly replied:
'The sort of weather that I like best.'

The walker, anxious for a better reply, asked again:
'All right, what type of weather is that?'
'I don't know yet!' replied the amused shepherd.
'But come on, how can you say that it will be the sort
of weather that you like?' retorted the walker drily, in a
less than philosophical spirit ...
The shepherd then added: 'In the course of my life,
I've come to see that I can't always get what I like,
so I decided to like what I am. That's the reason why
I'm sure that we're going to have the weather that I
like best ...'

If you wish to explore more deeply the theme of happiness, consult the _Petits cahiers d'exercices de Bienveillance envers soi-même, de Communication NonViolente®_ (Anne van Stappen) and _d'Entraînement au bonheur_ (Yves-Alexandre Thalmann).

Anne van Stappen is a doctor of medicine. After qualifying, she soon became very interested in human relations and trained in various therapeutic methods. Her desire to treat ailments of the body with words of the heart was realised when she discovered Non-Violent Communication (NVC). An NVC trainer since 1995, she presents at conferences and workshops on communication and conflict management. She has written *Don't Walk if You Can Dance*, *The Little Exercise Book of Being Kind to Yourself* and *The Little Exercise Book of Non-Violent Communication* (published by Jouvence).